Blown to Eter

the
Princess Irene
story

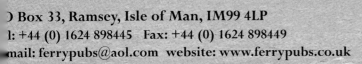

O Box 33, Ramsey, Isle of Man, IM99 4LP
l: +44 (0) 1624 898445   Fax: +44 (0) 1624 898449
mail: ferrypubs@aol.com   website: www.ferrypubs.co.uk

INTRODUCTION

The loss of the *Princess Irene* may seem a strange choice of subject to appear in the **Ferry Publications** book list but I make no apology for adding it to our increasing range of titles. Being raised and educated in the premier cross-Channel port of Dover, the name of her builders William Denny & Bros. of Dumbarton is synonymous with short-sea ships of the highest quality and so from the start the 'Irene' was a thoroughbred and came from the top stable of British yards. Secondly, having spent the first three years of my married life living and working in the Medway Towns, the name *Princess Irene* became increasingly familiar and regularly appeared in publications relating to Kent's largest river. Thirdly, a growing interest in the maritime activities of British Columbia was fostered following a first visit to the province in 1992.

From the start, my efforts at unearthing material concerning a ship which served for only the briefest of periods proved difficult and in spite of contacting all possible likely photographic sources in Britain and Canada, the Princess Irene *appears to have been a ship which was remarkably camera-shy. Even contemporary reports relating to the explosion which ended her tragically short career used photographs of her sister ship. In the circumstances, I too have had to resort to using views of the* Princess Margaret *although three rare pictures of the 'Irene' were fortunately located.*

Three classic Canadian works on Pacific Northwest shipping were consulted: "Those Beautiful Coastal Liners" by Robert D. Turner (Sono Nis Press, Victoria BC, 2001), "The Pacific Princesses" by Robert D. Turner (Sono Nis Press, Victoria BC, 1977) and "The Princess Story - A Century and a Half of West Coast Shipping" by Norman R. Hacking and W. Kaye Lamb (Mitchell Press Ltd., Vancouver BC, 1974). In England, Philip MacDougall's article "Death of a Princess" in "Coast and County" magazine (volume 10 number 3) proved to be a good introduction and was my first in-depth insight into the disaster. In addition, I have consulted documents relating to the ship from the Glasgow University Archives where Mr. George Gardner has been extremely helpful sifting through relevant correspondence and for locating the building contract, the Sheerness Library for contemporary newspaper reports and cuttings, the National Maritime Museum's outstation in the Brass Foundry at Woolwich Arsenal where all the Denny plans and photographic albums are housed and the Hydrographic Department of Medway Ports at Sheerness where Harbour Master Captain Peter White and River Services Manager Phil Woodgate continue to take a professional interest in the wreck. I would also like to thank the Royal Naval Museum at Portsmouth and its archivist Stephen Courtney, the staff at the BC Provincial Museum, Kelly-Ann Nolin and the BC Archives in Victoria, Phyllis Kelly of the Puget Sound Maritime Historical Association and the Medway Council Archives and Local Studies Centre at Strood. The Public Record Office at Kew houses several items of interest which were held as 'classified information' until 1966. These include the Official Enquiry into the ship's loss (ADM 1/8422/147), papers relating to diving operations on the wreck (ADM 1/8423/150), papers relating to finding a replacement ship (MT 23/376) and log books for March and April 1915 (ADM 53/55890 and 55891). A further document relates to Casualties (ADM 116/1445).

Finally, thanks are also due to John and Noreen Chambers, Bob Ratcliffe, Captain Mike Pryce, Robert D. Turner and David Parsons. As ever my friend and business partner, Miles Cowsill, provided valuable help involving layout and the manuscript's final production.

The Picture Library at London's National Maritime Museum is warmly thanked for its kind permission to reproduce the builders' rigging plan profile of Denny yard number 1006, as illustrated on the covers of this publication.

The book's title "Blown to Eternity" is taken from a headline which appeared in "The Guardian and East Kent Advertiser" on Saturday 29th May 1915.

John Hendy,
johnfhendy@hotmail.com
November 2001

The design for the **Princess Margaret** and **Princess Irene** was based on that of the Fairfield of Govan-built **Princess Charlotte** of 1908 which is seen alongside in Victoria. Sold out of CPR service in 1950, the ship saw further work in Greek waters as the **Mediterranean** before finally being broken up in 1964. *(British Columbia Archives B-06229)*

CANADIAN PACIFIC - NEW CENTURY, NEW SHIPS

During January 1901, the Canadian Pacific Railway Company (CPR) took a controlling interest in the Canadian Pacific Navigation Company and, under the watchful and visionary eye of its new manager Captain James Troop, looked to uprate and upgrade the ships and services then operated on the Canadian Northwest coast.

Traffic on the Canadian Pacific Railway's British Columbia Coast Service experienced a boom period in the years prior to World War 1 and so, in order to cater for the growing volumes of passengers and freight, the company ordered no fewer than seven new vessels. The near sisters *Princess Adelaide* and *Princess Alice* were built by Fairfield of Govan and Swan Hunter & Wigham Richardson respectively in 1910/11. The single-screwed, triple-expansion engined vessels were intended for the overnight service linking Vancouver with Victoria. They proved to be highly successful, both passing on to Greek owners Typaldos Bros. in 1949. Renamed *Angelika* and *Aegaeon,* they remained in service until the mid-60's.

The *Princess Mary* was also built in 1910 but by Bow, McLachlan & Co. of Paisley. This small coastal steamer worked the northern crossing of the Strait of Georgia (the stretch of water which separates mainland British Columbia from Vancouver Island) between Powell River and Comox. Two years later she was lengthened and served until 1952 when she was converted to become a barge.

A similar type of ship, the *Princess Sophia*, was built in the following year at the same Paisley yard as the 'Mary' for the Alaska service but sank with all hands on Vanderbilt Reef in 1918 while the *Princess Maquinna* of 1913 was the only one of the new vessels to be built locally by B.C. Marine Railways Co. Ltd. at Esquimalt, British Columbia. She was to serve the remote communities on the west coast of Vancouver Island and after forty reliable years she too was converted for use as a barge.

In addition to these five new vessels, in 1911 the Canadian Pacific Railway also acquired the *Princess Patricia* for the Vancouver - Nanaimo daylight route which she accomplished in a then unthinkable two hours. This vessel was built by William Denny & Bros. of Dumbarton in 1902. She was launched as the *Queen Alexandra* for Captain John Williamson's Turbine Steamers Ltd. for service in the Firth of Clyde. The *Queen Alexandra* followed the world's first turbine-driven passenger ship (the *King Edward*) and as such she was the first passenger vessel to reach the Pacific Northwest coast. She soon showed the advantages of turbine propulsion with her speed of 21.6 knots, vibration-free running and economy of fuel. Withdrawn from regular service in 1928, the popular ship remained on the CPR's books until 1937.

THE ORDER

In anticipation of the heavy traffic which would be generated by the forthcoming Panama-Pacific Exposition in 1915, on 24th May 1913 the CPR ordered twin turbine steam ships from the Dumbarton yard which, in close consultation with the engine's inventor Sir Charles Parsons, had pioneered the construction of turbine-driven passenger steamers.

Throughout its existence, the Leven Shipyard of William Denny & Bros. was noted for its skill in producing fast, shallow-draught vessels of lightweight construction. In the United Kingdom, an increasing number of railway companies were placing orders at the yard which continued in business until 1963.

Denny's had previously built the side-wheeled paddle steamer *Prince Rupert* (1,158 gross tons) for the Vancouver - Victoria service in 1894 but, due to the west coast politics of the day, she too was never to see the service for which she was built. Having reached Tenerife on her delivery voyage, the ship was ordered to return to the UK before eventually taking up service between Digby and Saint John on the Bay of Fundy in July 1895. The order for the new twin CPR ships was therefore not their first from Denny's but perhaps the success of the *Princess Patricia* and their pioneering work with steam turbine machinery was a contributory factor in the decision to return to the Leven Shipyard.

The new ships were named *Princess Margaret* (yard number 1005) and *Princess Irene* (yard number 1006) although it appears that the CPR had originally chosen the name *Princess Melita* for the second ship. As a vessel already existed with this name, the Board of Trade insisted on it being modified. The first ship was due to be delivered by 30th November 1914 while the second was due no later than 31st January 1915. The builders would be charged £50 a day for late delivery. Their dimensions were as follows:

Length overall:	395 ft.
Length at waterline:	390 ft.
Breadth:	54ft.
Draught:	17ft. 2 ins.
Displacement:	5,580 tons
Deadweight tons:	1,750 tons
Gross tons:	5,934 tons ('Margaret')
	5,932 tons ('Irene')
Net weight:	2,803 tons ('Margaret')
	2,793 tons ('Irene')

Cargo space:	48,110 cubic feet
First Class passengers:	437
Second Class passengers:	80
Bunker space:	495 tons of oil
Machinery (numbers 777-8):	Two shaft geared compound Parsons turbines 975 nhp 10 Babcock & Wilcox water tube boilers 202 lbs.

The ships were fitted with 77 First Class staterooms, 8 special staterooms and 42 other staterooms and a special observation room was fitted forward. Their dining rooms seated 160 passengers.

For safety purposes, for 71 ft. on either side of the boilers and 7

The world's second turbine passenger steamer, and the first such vessel in the Pacific Northwest, was the Denny of Dumbarton-built **Princess Patricia** (ex **Queen Alexandra**) of 1902 which entered service with the CPR in 1912. She was associated with the run between Nanaimo (Vancouver Island) and Vancouver and was not scrapped until 1937. (*British Columbia Archives D-01218*)

ft. in from the ships' side, a longitudinal bulkhead was fitted. All watertight doors could be shut automatically from the bridge and the ships were fitted with the latest wireless telegraphy. They were to carry 9 x 27ft. lifeboats and two sets of nested lifeboats (ie three lifeboats of diminishing size stored inside each other) while the owners were to supply one 24 ft. motor launch which was placed forward on the starboard side. The nested sets were the second group of lifeboats. In what was very much a sign of the changing times, both ships had special arrangements made to accommodate motor cars.

ACCOMMODATION AND ENGINES

Inspection of the ships' berthing plans at the National Maritime Museum's Woolwich Arsenal Brass Foundry outstation show that the passenger and crew accommodation was over five decks:

Boat Deck (A). Immediately behind the wheelhouse was the navigating officers' accommodation. The Captain's cabin was on the port side as were the cabins of the First Officer and Second Officer. On the starboard side and adjacent to the Captain's cabin were the Chart Room, then the Chief Officer and the Third Officer. Above the wheelhouse were the Flying Bridge and Tower Deck. Astern of the officers' cabins were First Class passenger staterooms, even numbers 2 - 42 on the starboard side while odd numbers 3 - 43 were on the port side. The six forward cabins (ie 2 - 7) were en-suite whilst the others were fitted with wash basins. Lavatories and bathrooms occupied the centre area of A Deck at the after end of which was the First Class Smoke Room. Photographs of the *Princess Margaret* in the Denny Collection show that this was beamed and timbered giving the impression of an old English country house. Lanterns hung from the deckhead and a brick-backed fireplace and coal fire served to give that

An interesting view of the ***Princess Margaret*** on the stocks before her launch at Dumbarton on 24th June 1914. Much of the after accommodation on the Boat Deck and Promenade Decks was removed in preparation for her minelaying role and two large mine ports were cut in the stern on the port and starboard quarters between her belting (rubbing strake) and her Upper Deck. *(National Maritime Museum, London. B7049)*

extra 'homely' ambience. Linking the forward cabin area to Deck B was the main companionway, illuminated by a domed glass roof below which was an ornate carving or moulding showing the Canadian Pacific Railway's CPR monogram and beaver emblem. Below this was a portrait of Mrs. R.M. Redmond who launched the ship at Dumbarton on 24th June 1914.

Promenade Deck (B). Below the wheelhouse was the First Class Observation Room and builders' photographs taken on board the 'Margaret' again show what an extremely elegant area this was. Two rows of comfortable wicker chairs faced outwards towards large panoramic windows, each with a semi-circular top. In the centre was a large writing table and deeply upholstered arm chairs. Above each window was a further elliptical window with stained glass patterns which not only gave the room added light but also extra height. The deckhead above was braced by Greek-style Corinthian columns. Cabins 45 - 127 were on the port side while 44 - 128 were starboard side cabins. Whilst all the cabins on A Deck were outside facing, the B Deck cabins were a mixture of inside and outside. The forwardmost cabins 44 - 51 were larger than the others. Just aft of the deck's centre point was a lounge which stretched across the entire width of the ship while at the after end was the First Class Bar.

Upper Deck (C). The Second Class Lounge was forward on this deck below the fo'c'sle. Aft of this was the First Class Vestibule with the Purser's Office and Chief Steward's cabin on the port side. Opposite these on the starboard side were the Barber's Shop and the Boot Room. Then cabins 129 - 201 occupied the port side whilst numbers 130 - 206 were on the starboard. The forward cabins, 129 - 137 and 130 - 138 were en-suite while adjacent to cabin 137 was the Official Room for meetings and conferences etc. Towards the after end

of C Deck were a Tea Room (port side) and a Writing Room (starboard side) while the Ladies' Lounge occupied the stern area.

Main Deck (D). In the area immediately below the bridge and the fo'c'sle were the Second Class lavatories while the Mail Room was on the starboard side forward. The largest area on this deck was occupied by freight space of which there was 30,300 cubic feet. Immediately astern of these were the galley, pantry, scullery, Butcher's shop, pantry, grill and Baker's shop all adjacent to the First Class Dining Room.

Orlop Deck (E). This comprised mainly of crew cabins and the Second Class Dining Room (port side) which was adjacent to the stewards' cabins. Further forward were the Second Class, seamen's and firemen's cabins. The centre area of this deck was the upper part of the engine room which was below on Deck F.

The ships were to be driven by two independent sets of Parsons compound steam turbines, each set comprising one High Pressure (HP) ahead turbine, one Low Pressure (LP) ahead turbine, one astern turbine and one set of gearing - each set driving one shaft and one manganese bronze propeller weighing 2 tons 17 cwt 3 qtrs. Their revolutions were to be about 280 per minute.

At 15 knots, 2.32 tons of oil an hour would be burned giving the ships 290 hours' steaming. At 18 knots 3.58 tons of oil would be used and the steaming time would drop to 187 hours. At 21 knots, 5.44 tons of oil an hour would be burned and only 123 hours of steaming would be given. At 22 knots, the oil burned would rise to 6.5 tons an hour but this would only permit the ship to sail 103 hours. The capacity of the oil fuel bunkers was 486.4 tons but this rose to 582.86 tons if the aft peak tanks were included.

The three funnels were double skinned, the inner one being about

2ft. smaller than the outer. The space was used for ventilating purposes drawing hot air away from their respective boilers and also alleyways and side cabins if required.

The twin ships were each to cost £196,896 10s. 0d. which was payable in five installments: 1) when the keel was laid, 2) when the vessel was framed, 3) when the vessel was plated, 4) when the vessel was launched and 5) when the vessel was handed over after satisfactory trials. The shipyard would make a handsome £5,639 10s. 0d. profit.

The ships were built to replace the reciprocating steamers *Princess*

The *Princess Irene* under construction at Denny's yard. Although the original print is of poor quality, the ship's superstructure is nearing completion and her paintwork is in an advanced state of preparation in readiness for her launch on 20th October 1914. *(British Columbia Archives 40799)*

Charlotte (1908-1950) and *Princess Victoria* (1903-1951). They were intended to surpass any tonnage then in service on the west coast and, although there were strong similarities between them and the Govan-built *Princess Charlotte*, they were considerably larger and faster and their fittings were magnificent.

THE CONTRACT

The contract between Denny and the CPR ran to seventeen pages and although much of this is taken up with the usual legal jargon, there are a number of interesting points which are worth mentioning. These not only amply illustrate the demanding nature of the ship owner but also the pressures which faced the ship builder.

It is stated that "all materials employed in the construction …shall be the best of their respective kinds. The workmanship throughout shall be of first class and of the most substantial character …" The company's representative would inspect all works in connection with the ships and would have the right to reject anything of which he disapproved concerning the quality of workmanship.

On their completion, trials were to be very rigorous and the first set consisted of a series of runs on the certified measured mile at Skelmorlie, two runs with and one against the tide at each of five different speeds - 15, 18, 20, 21.5 and 22.5 knots or upwards. During these trials the draught would be 16ft. maximum. It was stated that these runs were for the purpose of determining the revolutions in terms of speed.

The second set of tests comprised of helm, turning and astern trials. These were followed by a six hour run in the Firth of Clyde with 400 tons deadweight on board during which time "the mean revolutions … shall not be less than those ascertained from the

The *Princess Margaret* in the fitting-out basin at Denny's Dumbarton yard. The large panoramic windows of her First Class Observation Room can clearly be seen and the picture captures something of the energy and power of the ship's design. *(British Columbia Archives 60786)*

previous trials to be necessary to obtain 22.5 knots." If the average speed proved to be under 22.5 but not less than 22.25 knots, the builders would be expected to pay damages of £2,000. This would rise to £5,000 if the speed were between 22.25 and 22 knots and £12,000 if under 22 knots but above 21.75 knots. Should the speed drop to less than 21.75 knots then the CPR could not only refuse to take delivery but also expect a full repayment from Denny. The six hour trial burning Texas oil was not expected to exceed 7.5 tons per hour and a fine of £1,500 was to be payable for every ton used over the stipulated amount.

Canadian Pacific's London representative was Major H. Maitland Kersey, DSO and much of the surviving documentation between Denny's and the railway company (held in the Glasgow University Archives) is addressed to him at 8 Waterloo Place.

On 29th July 1913, only two months after the order, Denny's were writing to Major Kersey concerning a meeting held in London some five days previously. Present were none other than Sir Charles Parsons and Sir John H. Biles when the question concerning the type of turbine machinery to be used in the ships was fully discussed and a cablegram was sent to Montreal for a final decision to be made. It was decided to proceed with the very new geared turbines but during the course of the conversation Sir Charles stated that if best economy at 17 knots in service, corresponding approximately to half power, were an object then he would recommend either the addition of cruising stages to the high pressure turbines or that the high pressure turbines should be left as originally designed, and for each shaft a separate cruising turbine should be provided. To suit both cases then the low pressure turbines would have to be modified.

Major Kersey instructed Denny's to look further into this question with Sir Charles Parsons as he needed to know details of the extra weight and the costs involved. Sir Charles informed the shipyard that due to the slightness of the gain of the second proposal over the first he advised the second be abandoned. Denny's found that the engine room space would allow for the adaptation, its extra weight being 8 tons per vessel and its extra cost some £1,200 for each ship. Sir Charles estimated that the economy at half power due to this scheme as compared with ordinary geared turbines would be 10%.

Denny's went on to plead that they required the decision to be made "as soon as possible" as owing to the delay in the trials of the London Brighton & South Coast Railway's *Paris,* they were already later than anticipated in getting under way with the work.

The letter concluded by stating that as the designs of the heating surface had proceeded so far, they would rather leave matters as they were but should the CPR decide to reduce the surface from 34,000 to 33,000 sq. ft. then there would be credits in their favour of 8 tons and £390.

The final costs of the handsome sisters were in excess of their contract prices. The 'Margaret' cost some £203,448.10s. 0d. (this working out as £7.60 per ton) of which the hull cost £132,562 and machinery £60,383 while the 'Irene' was slightly cheaper at £202,690.12s. 6d. (£7.55 a ton). Her hull cost £125,496 while machinery cost £55,847. Denny's made profits of £7,215 10s. 0d on the first ship and, due to the great savings made, as much as £14,773 on the *Princess Irene*.

LAUNCHES AND TRIALS

With war in Europe growing ever closer, on 24th June 1914 the

This wonderful view of the **Princess Margaret** on trials in the Firth of Clyde in October 1914 amply illustrates the superb Troop-inspired design of the twin steamers. The CPR houseflag is flying from the mainmast and the ship glistens from stem to stern in the autumn sunshine. *(National Maritime Museum, London. B7046)*

Another magnificent trials photograph of the beautiful **Princess Margaret** on the Skelmorlie measured mile *(British Columbia Archives 16929)*

Princess Margaret was launched with all due ceremony by Mrs. R.M. Redmond, the daughter of the CPR's president Sir Thomas Shaughnessy, who was then in Britain on her honeymoon. Once in her element, the ship was nudged to the adjacent fitting-out basin by two paddle tugs, the *Flying Dutchman* on the bow, where she was completed before leaving the yard for trials on 16th October. Here, in

This view of mines stored on their rails is believed to have been taken later in the war in the requisitioned and converted New Zealand passenger steamer HMS **Wahine**. It gives a fair indication of the claustrophobic conditions on the mine decks. *(Royal Naval Museum, Portsmouth.)*

an inclement Firth of Clyde, she attained a speed of 23.113 knots over the measured mile using 15,365 shp at 286.7 rpm. During the six hour trial she made 22.71 knots with 14,158 shp with engines running at 278.6 rpm.

Trials photographs show what a superb-looking specimen the *Princess Margaret* really was. In the opinion of this present writer, the 1914 twins were the most beautiful 'Princess' ships ever constructed for the CPR. With almost vertical stems, three elegantly placed funnels of equal height between two lofty masts of identical rake and modern cruiser sterns - the first 'Princess' class ships to be so fitted - the 'Margaret' and her unlucky sister were a sheer delight to the eye. In line with their Canadian Pacific fleet companions, there was very little flare of the bow in order to prevent damage while berthing in any weather conditions while the majority of cargo was to be loaded through large freight doors straight from the quayside onto their Main Decks.

But all was not well during this period as the 'Margaret' suffered from excessive vibration at high speeds and so additional stiffening, particularly in the shaft tunnels, was fitted which seemed to solve the problem. She was delivered to her owners on 15th November but did not immediately sail for her home base at Victoria BC due to concerns over the movements of Vice Admiral Graf von Spee's East Asiatic Squadron.

Only two weeks earlier, at the very one-sided Battle of Coronel (off the coast of Chile), von Spee had out-gunned, out-run and out-fought the ancient British cruisers HMS *Good Hope* and HMS *Monmouth*. His armoured cruisers *Scharnhorst* and *Gneisenau* with their light cruiser escorts were in the process of making their way back to Germany and would in all likelihood be somewhere in the South

Atlantic at the same time as the passenger steamer was sailing south to round the Horn. Although the Panama Canal had opened for traffic in August 1914, it appears to have been the CPR's intention to steam the new ships to Victoria on the traditional route. It was later suggested that the twins might accompany each other on the long voyage to the Pacific Northwest coast.

By the time that the German squadron was eventually sunk by the might of the battle cruisers HMS *Invincible* and HMS *Inflexible* and their accompanying cruisers at the Battle of the Falkland Islands on 8th December 1914, the fate of the CPR sisters at Dumbarton was also in the process of being sealed.

The *Princess Irene* followed her sister into the River Leven on 20th October 1914. With the war now underway, the pomp and ceremony usually associated with ship launches was perhaps inappropriate and the fact that she was launched by Mrs. J.A. Heritage, the wife of the Chief Engineer of the *Princess Margaret,* appears to indicate that large numbers of Canadian guests did not wish to risk the sea journey to Europe. Sadly no photographs of the launch or subsequent trials exist in the Denny Collection at the National Maritime Museum.

The *Princess Irene's* trials, which commenced on 15th January 1915, were operated with a set of three and then four-bladed propellers. On the first measured mile runs, with the three-bladed screws, she reached 22.9 knots. Then, fitted with the four-bladed set, on 25th January on the measured mile she bettered her sister by making 23.333 knots with fewer engine revolutions (281 rpm) and less shaft horse power (14,873). As has occurred so often with identical sister ships, the second vessel again proved to be the faster but Dr. W. Kaye Lamb, co-author of "The Princess Story - a Century and a Half of West Coast Shipping" wrote that the papers of John A.

Heritage (1866-1958 and who was at this time the Chief Engineer of the *Princess Margaret*) showed that careful study of the ship's performance indicated the three-bladed propellers were actually more efficient, especially at lower speeds.

MINE WARFARE AND CONVERSIONS

Prior to the outbreak of war on 4th August 1914, mines and minelaying were still a comparatively new facet of sea warfare and mine technology was constantly being modified.

Early the following morning the crew of a fishing boat in the Thames estuary reported that they had seen an unknown steamer 'throwing things overboard' about 20 miles north east of the Outer Gabbard and the light cruiser HMS *Amphion* was sent to investigate. She eventually came upon the two funnelled Heligoland excursion vessel *Konigin Luise* which had been converted for her new role within a space of 12 hours - so quickly in fact that her twin 3.4 inch guns had been left on the quayside in Germany. Realising that there was no escape, the passenger steamer scuttled herself and the *Amphion* later picked up survivors. Returning to Harwich the next day the light cruiser became an early casualty of the war when she broke her back after striking one of the 'Luise's' mines.

It was appreciated by the Royal Navy that, for their own minelaying measures, high speed ships were required to reach the area to be mined, lay the mines during the hours of darkness and escape from the scene before possible detection. Although there were a number of suitable British cross-Channel steamers which would have been ideal for this task in terms of speed, they were all hampered by their lack of size. The Admiralty considered that the new Canadian Pacific steamers would be ideal for the role, their size and speed making them extremely useful additions to HM Fleet.

Accordingly, on 26th December 1914 ('Margaret') and 20th January 1915 ('Irene') the ships were requisitioned by the Admiralty and were gutted in preparation for their conversion. In addition to storage bays for up to 400 mines, both sisters were fitted with two 4.7 inch guns, two 3 inch guns, anti-aircraft guns and smaller armaments. In their new role they each carried a complement of 225 officers and crew.

A document dated 19th February 1915, in the Glasgow University Archives, ponderously entitled "'*Princess Irene*' List of work removed from ship and stored as stated hereafter in this list" gives a detailed insight into the work involved when all the ship's luxurious fittings were removed and stored ready for the time when she would return to the yard and reclaim them:-

"Promenade Deck State Rooms, Upper Deck State Rooms, Smoke Room, Ladies' Lounge, American Bar, Dining Saloon, Galley, Engineers' accommodation. Framing and panelling for same, main stairs aft and balustrading now stored in protected shed in works.

Plumbers' pipes and sanitary pipes, hot and cold water fittings to staterooms that have been removed, also heating pipes for same rooms also stored in locked-up shed in yard, but we are not able to particularise positions but some have been carefully numbered, so that they can be replaced if found undamaged when the vessel is being refitted.

All the above to be subject to the Company's representative's inspection.

The ship's fittings, pictures, mirrors, plumbers' fittings for baths, wash basins etc., also electrical fittings, upholstery furnishings, joiners' furnishings, pictures for special rooms, Mr. Crawley's pictures, are stored carefully in our General Store mostly in boxes.

The boats and davits removed from the vessel are stored in our Barge Park.

The above materials will go back so far as are found fit to be used again but we are of the opinion that a very large percentage of the woodwork has been considerably damaged in removing and will not be suitable for replacing in the vessel when refitting takes place.

The value agreed upon between the Company's Inspector and ourselves in the estimated value for the woodwork removed from the ship and the wages expended on the manufacture of same, but not for the erecting of this work on board while building, amounts to:-

Woodwork and wages	about £6,500
and the furnishings as enumerated	£3,500
	£10,000."

The damage to the *Princess Irene's* wooden panelling is of interest as it indicates the speed at which she was gutted and converted. It is difficult to imagine that, given an adequate amount of time, those craftsmen who were responsible for installing the wooden panels would not have removed them with the same care and pride as they had placed them in position just weeks earlier. The damage seems to show that in their haste to strip the ship of her combustible fittings, the panels were simply ripped from their mountings.

The *Princess Irene* was delivered on 26th January 1915 (just six days after being requisitioned) and following her conversion she finally left the River Clyde for her new base at Sheerness (Kent) on 18th March 1915.

Although no plans appear to exist showing the nature of the conversion work, the study of photographs, before and after, gives a good indication of the modifications made.

The Upper Deck (Deck C) and the Main Deck (Deck D) must have been completely cleared. Deck D consisted mainly of freight space but astern of it were the ship's main galley and the First Class Dining Room. Internal bulkheads were removed on both decks and rails were installed so that the mines could be manoeuvred towards the stern where large minelaying ports were cut on both port and starboard quarters. The after end of the Boat Deck (Deck A) was cut away in the area of the First Class Smoke Room and the appearance of twin derricks indicates that a hatch had been cut through the Promenade Deck (Deck B) in order that the new and deadly cargo could be lowered directly into the void spaces below where the mines were stored and primed. An after bridge was also constructed although it is probable that this was for the purpose of overseeing the loading of mines rather than for navigational purposes.

Built alongside the CPR sisters at Denny's Dumbarton yard was the South Eastern & Chatham Railway turbine steamer *Biarritz* (2,495 gross tons, yard number 1015). Launched in December 1914, and intended for the Dover - Calais link, she too was taken over as a fast minelayer, leaving the yard in this role in the following March. Then there was the London Brighton & South Coast Railway's *Paris* (1,774 gross tons, yard number 973) which was launched during April 1913 and sailed in July for service on the Newhaven - Dieppe route but which at the outbreak of war was ripe for conversion. The Union Steamship Company of New Zealand later provided their *Wahine* (4,436 gross tons, yard number 971). She had left the yard for Wellington in May 1913 but returned to the theatre of war to assist firstly as a despatch ship in the Gallipoli campaign and then from July 1916 as part of the minelaying measures as a direct replacement for the *Princess Irene*. Documents in the Public Record Office show that the efforts to find a replacement commenced as early as the afternoon of the *Princess Irene's* destruction.

OFFICERS

The man appointed to be the Master of the *Princess Irene* was Captain Mervyn H. Cobbe. He had entered the Navy as a cadet in January 1886 being promoted to Commander in 1904 (the year of his marriage) and rising to Captain in 1911.

His second in command and Chief Officer was Thomas H.M. Maurice who had entered the Service in January 1891 and had been promoted to the rank of Commander in December 1908.

The First Officer was Lieutenant-Commander Humphrey R. Cottrell-Dormer. He was born in April 1881 and was the eighth son of the late owner of Rousham Hall in Oxfordshire. The Second Officer was Lieutenant Colin G. Harper while the Third Officer was Lieutenant Charles B. Wiatt, RNR.

The ship's engineers were all acting in a temporary capacity and all RNR officers. The Chief Engineer was Mr. James Wallace who had been appointed to that post by the CPR and had decided to remain on board during the ship's period with the Royal Navy. The two Senior Engineers were Henry J. Shee and Stanley Reed while the other three senior officer engineers were W. W. Rennie, Peter Stewart and William Galletly. In addition there were no fewer than nine Temporary Assistant Engineers one of whom was The Hon. Cormac F. Deane-Morgan, the fourth son of Lord Muskerry of Springfield Castle in County Limerick.

THE *BULWARK* DISASTER

At 07.35 on Thursday 26th November 1914, the pre-Dreadnought battleship HMS *Bulwark* of the 5th Battle Squadron blew

The **Princess Irene** at anchor in the River Medway with HMS **Paris** ahead. This view clearly shows the ports in her stern which allowed mines from the Main Deck to be laid but less obvious are the mine doors right at the stern on the deck above (Upper Deck). Notice too the crossed derricks (used for loading the mines) with the new quarter deck at the after end of the Boat Deck and the foreshortening of the the accommodation on the Promenade Deck in order to allow the mounting of the after guns. The Upper Deck's after open promenade has been plated in. *(Puget Sound Maritime Historical Association. 6865)*

up without warning at her moorings at No.17 buoy in Kethole Reach on the River Medway.

The *London* class ship had been built at Devonport Dockyard in 1902 and was of some 15,000 tons. After spending the night ashore, many of the ship's complement of 741 had returned to the *Bulwark* in time for breakfast while on the quarter deck the ship's band was playing. It was a quiet morning which was suddenly shattered when an explosion followed immediately by a huge vertical sheet of flame and debris rent the calm Kentish air. More explosions followed and once the thick grey enveloping volumes of cloud had cleared away, there was little trace of the once-proud *Bulwark*. The explosion was heard 20 miles away in Whitstable while Sheerness and nearby Rainham suffered blast damage before the broken remnants of the ship rained down on them. There were just 12 survivors.

The Court of Enquiry heard that there was no evidence of an external explosion and everything pointed to an internal catastrophic magazine detonation although there was no proof of its actual cause.

Surely, it was impossible that lightning could strike twice on the same river ?

TO WAR!

The *Princess Irene's* period of commission was to last just over two months and during late April she laid her first batch of 280 mines within sight of the chalk ramparts of Beachy Head in East Sussex.

Following the success of the enemy's bombardments of Great Yarmouth, West Hartlepool, Scarborough and Whitby in November and December 1914, early British minelaying exercises involved the laying of protective barrages off the east coast but before long measures were also taken to prevent the German High Seas Fleet from making sorties into the North Sea. Accordingly, during early May an interception minefield was laid north west of the island of Heligoland when the *Princess Margaret* and *Princess Irene*, escorted by the Harwich Force's light cruiser HMS *Aurora* and two divisions of destroyers from Harwich, began the dangerous work. On this occasion the 'Irene' laid as many as 470 mines.

THE THIRD OPERATION

The majority of the *Princess Irene's* mines were in all probability brought down the River Medway by barges from Upnor where there was a special mooring for mine-carrying lighters. The Royal Navy's Chattenden & Upnor Railway would have delivered them from the Lodge Hill ammunition stores and in preparation for their arrival, on Tuesday 25th May the *Princess Irene* was moved from her moorings off Sheerness Dockyard to a quieter anchorage at No. 28 buoy in Saltpan Reach on the other side of the river and well away from any settlement. This in itself was recognition that the act of loading and priming mines was a very dangerous operation. The design of mines then in use had been finalised in the previous year and they appear to have been of a type known as the Vickers-Elia, or simply V.E. They each weighed 760 kg, were mostly contact mines charged with high-explosive and were activated by a swinging arm at their base rather than by a series of 'horns.' If the mine were struck by a passing ship, the arm would release the firing striker which would cause detonation.

The arming devices then in use were Heneage 'pistols' which required a striker pin to be 'cocked' using a compression spring before loading and therein lay the Achilles heel of this pistol type. They were surrounded by soft plugs that dissolved after a short period in the water at which time the mines theoretically became 'active.' It can be appreciated that arming mines at this period was both risky and potentially unsafe. In the case of a defective 'pistol,' detonation of the charge was inevitable but the Navy was very much aware of the problem and safer designs were at that time waiting to be introduced.

Lieutenant Graham Wragge of HMS *Pembroke* was in the chart house of the Mine Carrier HMS *Cove* which was loading mines into HMS *Angora* at the time of the explosion. He stated that the *Princess Irene's* mines were a mixture of about 90 liddite (which had been sent from Woolwich about 48 hours previously), a few ammonia but the majority were guncotton. The pistols in use were all of the Mark III or Mark II* types which were about to be replaced by the safer Mark IV variety.

With the unarmed mines remaining in their adjacent barges overnight, at 06.00 on Wednesday 26th May the process began of lifting them on board. Once stored on its mine rail, each had its cover removed before being skillfully fitted with a detonator and primer. The pistols were firstly 'cocked' before being handed to the priming party who fitted them with their detonators into the mines. It was planned to complete the task of priming on the following day.

COUNT DOWN TO DISASTER

On Thursday 27th May, the crew of the *Princess Irene* were not the only personnel on board. A party of Sheerness Dockyard workers had been undertaking some refit work for at least three weeks previously and arrived on board from their steam pinnace, or 'trot' boat, at about 07.00. The work was fairly 'immediate' for it had involved night shifts and earlier in the week a party of men had been brought down from Chatham Dockyard to assist in its completion. This was due to be

finished by 25th May and a later report from the Senior Officer in charge of the Mining Committee stated that by then it had been hoped that the mine rails would be completed and so there is some evidence to suggest that the *Princess Irene's* minelaying capacity was actually in the process of being increased. There was also seemingly some important business to discuss as that morning the Captain-in-Charge of Minelayers, Engineer Lieutenant Reed RNR, Assistant Paymaster Stallard and some ratings from the *Princess Margaret* who had accompanied the Captain-in-Charge were also on board. Acting Mate W.B. Sinclair with a working party of 88 Petty Officers and men from the Chatham Depot were on the mine decks assisting with the priming while Steam Launch *263* with an Acting Mate and a crew of five was lying alongside. The sailing barge *Messenger* was also alongside collecting the discarded mine covers which were being thrown into her forward hold through the open cargo doors in the 'Irene's' shell-plating.

At about 09.15 Chief Petty Officer Thomson (the ship's Chief Steward), AB William Paice (acting as ship's postman) and Signalman John Sutton went ashore. Sutton was to visit the dentist on an outing which he would not normally consider fortunate.

It was a very brisk morning with a stiff breeze blowing cold and clear continental air in from the north east. The cloudless sky was brilliantly blue and the tide was on the flood swinging the stern of the *Princess Irene* round to face the south west.

At 11.10 Mr. Stephen Quint, who was in charge of the shipwrights belonging to the Chief Constructor's Department working on the refit aboard the vessel, boarded Steam Launch *122* with a group of five Dockyard workers who had been removing slings for testing ashore. They were also on their way to attend a medical to check for an outbreak of 'spotted fever.' Quint had arrived on board the minelayer at 10 o'clock that morning to inspect the work and, with his job completed, he had left for the shore. The remainder of the 76 local men and boys remained on board.

At 11.14, disaster overtook the *Princess Irene* which was sitting on her moorings west south west of Port Victoria pier in the River Medway's Saltpan Reach.

Without any apparent warning, there was a tremendous explosion which one eye-witness likened to an eruption of Mount Vesuvius. The shock waves rattled and shook houses in the nearby town of Sheerness which lay E.N.E. across the river just 3 miles away. Where seconds previously the new ship had bobbed peacefully on her moorings with an empty barge and 'trot' boat *263* alongside, columns of ugly flames and smoke seared into the spring sky. And when the flames had subsided, a vast pall of white smoke hung suspended above the river.

The ship had completely disappeared and the waters of the Medway were a cluttered mass of floating wreckage.

EYE-WITNESS ACCOUNTS

The nearest witness was probably Edward Standen who was returning to Sheerness on 'trot' boat *122* and facing the *Princess Irene*. He said that the flash covered the entire ship but felt that it originated in the forward part and ran towards the stern.

Leading Signalman William Grimsey also saw it happen. He was standing on the converted British India Steam Navigation Co's HMS *Angora* (1911-1932) which like the 'Irene' had been requisitioned for minelaying duties earlier that year. She was moored up river from the *Princess Irene* and Grimsey was in the process of signalling the Torpedo

School at Sheerness (HMS *Actaeon II*). With the *Princess Irene* directly in his line of sight, he later described seeing a flash which seemed to come from the midships section followed by a terrific explosion.

Another witness spoke of a tongue of fire shooting up about 20 ft. above the ship followed instantly by a gigantic upheaval and an

The only known picture of the **Princess Irene** in operation on her second minelaying sortie in early May 1915. The photograph was taken from the stern of the light cruiser HMS **Aurora** and the ship is being escorted by destroyers of the Harwich Force. It is of interest that the ship retains her CPR black hull and white upperworks. Her lifeboats are swung out and she appears to be heading northwards off the Suffolk coast. *(National Maritime Museum, London. N22793)*

enormous column of smoke. After an interval of several seconds, the blast of the explosion swept across the river with terrific force. When the smoke pall thinned sufficiently, he told the "Guardian and East Kent Advertiser," there was nothing left of the *Princess Irene*.

Steam launches and Admiralty tugs came at full speed to the scene of the disaster but hopes of saving the lives of any survivors were grimly disappointed. The ship had simply disappeared.

W. G. Moore wrote about his experiences in the book "Early Bird" published by Putnam in 1963. He was standing on the Air Station slipway at Grain, just a few hundred yards from the *Princess Irene*. Moore wrote, "The whole thing was too awe-inspiring for me to appreciate the horror of it immediately. It started with stabs of flame spurting up from her deck from stem to stern, then a colossal roar and everything was hurled into the air - superstructure, hatches, deckplates, boats, men and debris and a column of smoke went up to a mushroom head at about 1,200 feet. Papers and light debris were picked up seven miles down wind. The forces of such an explosion seem to work in a parabolic curve and I was too close to get the full strength of the blast. I was blown onto my back but not stunned. The aeroplane hangar doors behind me were all blown in and pieces of plate from the ship's side were found half a mile away in the marshes beyond the aerodrome."

A further Dockyard employee, Mr. Kilpatrick, was with his colleague Mr. Hodges on their way out to the *Princess Irene* in a pinnace. He told "The Sheerness Times," "We were lying on the cushions in the cabin when the explosion occurred. Hodges was shaken onto the floor by the concussion and we both ran out to ascertain what had happened. But the rain of debris was so thick that we were compelled to seek shelter in the cabin and when we were able to emerge again there was no sign of the *Princess Irene* upon which we had been working only a few hours before. The scene was extraordinary immediately after the accident. The ship appeared to have been blown into minute fragments, many of which seemed to hang in the air burning. The force of the explosion was vertical and a pall of black and white smoke hovered high over the spot for some minutes and then began to drift away in almost a solid mass. There was little or no disturbance to the water but the surface was quickly covered in a litter of wreckage. This was so small that it was just as if you had emptied a box of matches into a bath and it was a difficult matter to drive our boat through it.... We saw nothing of the men who had been on the ship and the largest pieces of her which we noticed were a portion of the mast dipping through the waves and a part of the hull. For the rest there were just these charred splinters and burnt mattresses and items of that nature littering the waters."

On the dockside, a horrified CPO Thomson waiting to return to his vessel saw a flash which seemed to envelop the whole ship.

Master-at-Arms John Allum on board HMS *Angora* was thrown off his feet by the explosion. He ran forward to the forecastle and saw a mine descend to the water about 6 ft. from the starboard side of his ship. Fortunately it did not explode.

Lieutenant Arthur Notley was on board HM Trawler *Scott* about 3.25 cables away from the 'Irene.' He said that the explosion occurred by her mainmast, well abaft of her funnels. This was a yellowish white flame which rose to about 60 ft. and was accompanied by a dense volume of dark brown smoke that completely and suddenly enveloped the vessel. Between three and five seconds later there was a second, dull, explosion, quite distinct from the first, and this time there was no flame but a large amount of white smoke rising inside a column of

Left: The death of the ***Princess Irene***. This remarkable photographic montage was one of a series of three submitted as evidence at the ***Princess Irene*** enquiry and stamped "Secret." They were taken by Lieutenant HWD Griffiths RN of Torpedo Boat *112* in Stangate Creek, about 1 mile due south of the ***Princess Irene's*** anchorage. The caption states that the picture was taken 45 seconds after the explosion. Two other photographs, exposed a few minutes later, are from a higher angle, looking across the stern of the ship in the foreground, and show the smoke column drifting away to the south west. *(Public Record Office, London. ADM1/8422/147)*

black smoke which assumed a much greater altitude. By this time the ship was totally obscured and he could see no more. The two explosions were connected by a continuous series of small explosions sounding like machine gun fire which continued for another four seconds after the second major explosion. Notley surmised that this was the sound of bursting rivets. The *Scott* was showered with pieces of broken metal and rivets, one piece weighing about 80 lbs tearing and breaking up the after bridge.

A writer describing himself as "An Onlooker" provided another moving description of the death of the *Princess Irene* which he witnessed from the Rainham Road. "A flash of flame was followed by a huge column of smoke and vapour, which shot skywards. This rose higher and changed from a dense black at the water's surface, through all the paler shades of grey as it ascended. At a height of two miles or more, the gases assumed the form of a glorious towering pile of snow-white cumulus cloud which resembled the centre of a mighty cauliflower, the dark trailing stem of which reached down to the water as if anchored there."

Lieutenant J.B. Manners was attached to HMS *Actaeon II*, the Sheerness Torpedo School, and was standing on the poop deck just a few hundred yards away from the 'Irene.' He described hearing a sharp report followed by a terrific explosion. A large mass of flame went up to a great height, then seemed to stop and burst into flame again. "Flame, gas and smoke were flying upwards and I saw many fragments of debris and wreck flying horizontally across the water in all directions. I was particularly struck by the terrific height that some of the payment went in a huge column of vapourish gas all fiercely aflame." The smoke went up two miles, as later 'verified by trigonometry.' Manners had also seen the *Bulwark* explosion and believed the destruction of the 'Irene' to be worse. Perhaps it was Manners who also spoke to a special correspondent of "The Times" on the evening of the tragedy. He was on the Sheerness side of the vessel and as the wind was blowing strongly in the opposite direction, he was able clearly to observe the explosion which was the most extraordinary experience of his life. The *Princess Irene* seemed to be hurled into the air a mile high in 10,000 fragments. He could distinctly make out the forms of men amidst the flying wreckage and the great cloud of smoke. The end of the vessel was appallingly sudden and complete.

Manners was ordered by his Commanding Officer to go to the scene of the disaster in Steam Launch *161* but found only fragments of wreckage and mattresses. After his lunch Manners was again out in the river sweeping for obstructions in the vicinity of the wreck. "I caught several obstructions and buoyed them and made repeated soundings just before and after low water." He reported that a portion of the forepart of the *Princess Irene* was still attached to No.28 buoy by its cable and was awash at low tide.

In nearby Sheerness, life in the town came to an instant halt. After the *Bulwark* disaster the previous November, everyone knew that something dreadful had occurred. Within seconds the column of smoke rose above the roof tops and indicated the location of the explosion. The smoke pillar remained for some minutes before it started to disperse but over the water a dense haze of pungent smoke obscured the empty mooring.

THE AFTERMATH

The cataclysmic explosion distributed fragments of the broken *Princess Irene* over a wide area but there was no apparent order or pattern to the rain of broken debris which now descended on the surrounding river and countryside. Neither did the ship's scattered remains appear to originate from any pre-ordained place within her recently ordered interior. Instead they represented the disordered and chaotic remnants of a once-proud ship. Whilst heavier materials plunged straight back to earth, the lighter scraps fluttered on the breeze to land later both silently and unnoticed.

Falling metal hit the Navy's oil tanks at the nearby Isle of Grain Fuel Depot causing four of them to rupture and spill their viscous contents across a wide area. The pumping station and the main pipeline were put out of action due to fragments of the ship's side falling on them.

In Grain village a nine year old girl, Hilda Johnson, was killed in the garden of her uncle and aunt when a piece of falling metal struck her on the head. This was later produced as evidence at the Coroner's court where it was noted that one side showed evidence of fusion due to the tremendous heat generated by the detonation.

George Bradley, aged 47, was a farm labourer at work in a field at Home Farm near Grain when the explosion occurred. The shock killed him. Victor Potter, an electrical fitter, was on duty on the bridge of the Fleet Coaling Ship *C8* which was about half a mile from the *Princess Irene*. A falling piece of steel plate some 42 inches long and 6 inches wide pierced the chart house causing him fatal head injuries. A part of one of the 'Irene's' ten boilers landed on the deck, injuring two other men and toppling a deck crane.

At Detling (11 miles distant) paper fragments eventually fell from the sky while at Hollingbourne (12 miles) the blast blew open the doors and windows of the village school. Other windows were broken at Milton and Newington (both 6 miles) while a number of local hay stacks were set alight.

There was reported panic at Chatham (8 miles) as many thought that the blast had come from the town's Dockyard. Doors and windows were rattled and smashed, the church ceiling at Lower Halstow (4 miles) fell in, a box of butter fell on Bredhurst (9 miles) while fragments of charred wood were dropped onto nearby Grain village. A local newspaper report stated that the bang was louder than that which had come from the *Bulwark* and it was even heard in the county town of Maidstone (13 miles) where windows were broken and bottles and jars were jolted from shelves.

Arthur Wade from Rainham (6 miles due SW) received a telephone message from his wife telling him that in their neighbour's garden had just fallen a boot, a man's collar and a pound of butter. Elsewhere in the village, photographs, a tablecloth and serviettes were discovered and the local police conducted a house-to-house enquiry asking people to search their gardens for human remains. One local resident described the thousands of bits and pieces from the fall-out as looking like confetti. Farm workers scoured local orchards and fields searching for limbs, heads and other broken body parts.

In Sittingbourne (6 miles), people heard the explosion and some windows fell in yet most believed that their town's railway station was under attack from enemy aeroplanes. Then the pall of smoke from the direction of the River Medway indicated that something far more sinister had occurred.

Along the Lower Rainham Road, which stretches along the creeks and saltings south west of where the *Princess Irene* was lying, a number of towels and a sailor's jumper were picked up while a piece of charred wood, about thirty inches long and apparently a piece of cabin panelling, was discovered. Three miles beyond the village and in the direction a Maidstone, a bundle of papers was found and nearby, a tin of condensed milk.

On the marshes nearby the mooring, the body of a seaman was found and lying across his head was the jacket sleeve of a naval Lieutenant.

The adjacent 400 ft. long Port Victoria railway pier and station were badly damaged as exploding metal fragments embedded themselves into stout wooden piling which had stood the ravages of wind and tide for 32 years.

Such was the nature and intensity of the disaster which had overtaken the *Princess Irene* that few bodies were found and most of those recovered in one piece were badly burned or mutilated. Human remains were recovered from a wide area and by late on Thursday night only three bodies out of about four hundred had been brought ashore.

It was not until 18.20 on the evening of the disaster that the Navy posted their first official notice on the Dockyard gate. It briefly read, "It is much regretted that the following workmen, as far as can be ascertained, have lost their lives while in the execution of their duty at Sheerness." The notice and its list of names was signed by Rear

Admiral R. J. Prendergast, the Superintendent of Sheerness Dockyard.

Over the following days the scattered remains of the dead were brought to the Royal Naval Hospital at Gillingham where numbered coffins were lined up in an effort to identify their gruesome contents. Whilst tattoos sufficed for some, others carried laundry marks on their clothing while Dockyard requisition slips highlighted the bodies of the local Sheerness workers.

The Chatham Coroner reported that identification would have been easier had the seamen worn identity tags around their necks but the 'Irene's' crew had been superstitious and had refused to wear them. The disaster had a far more pronounced effect on the town of Sheerness than had the destruction of HMS *Bulwark* in November 1914. Although the *Bulwark* lost almost 750 men, she was moored much further up river towards Chatham and her crew was mainly Portsmouth-based. In the case of the *Princess Irene*, 76 local Dockyard workers had been on board and in the close community of narrow streets around the Dockyard's perimeter wall, everyone was deeply affected. In Granville Road alone, there were ten bereaved families.

As after the disaster which had earlier befallen HMS *Bulwark*, local rumour was rife although with the experience of hindsight after the loss of the battleship, an internal explosion due to an incorrectly primed mine seemed to be the most obvious answer to the question "Why?"

The final anchorage. The view northwards from the preserved paddle steamer **Kingswear Castle** in Stangate Creek looking towards Thamesport in May 2001. The **Princess Irene's** wreck buoy (ZI) is immediately to the right of the right hand crane and below the two adjacent chimneys. Grain Power Station is on the far right, opposite the town of Sheerness. *(John Hendy)*

THE SURVIVOR

There was just one survivor. Stoker David Wills of the Chatham Depot's working party was serving as a cook and was going for an early lunch in the forward galley at the time of the explosion. He was rescued from the water by the crew of the tug *Bruno* which was just 50 yards away, his memory a total blank concerning the circumstances of how he came to be there.

After the smoke and falling fragments had cleared, one of the tug's crew spotted the fortunate Wills struggling in the river amidst wreckage and oil. The Master, Mr. Pilcher, immediately swung his vessel round and, by reaching over the bow, the tug's stoker managed to drag the oil-smothered survivor on board and transfer him to the adjacent *Angora*.

Wills received terrible burns to his face, arms and hands from which he never really recovered and he carried his physical and mental scars throughout the rest of his life. After a prolonged convalescence at the Naval Hospital in Chatham, as soon as he was fit for duty he rejoined the Navy where he completed a further 12 years' service. In an interview with the "Sheerness Times & Guardian" in December 1995, his son Ronald related how his father could never forget the sight of bodies raining down and that he became terrified of thunderstorms. "He would remember the men who died, blown to pieces, their limbs scattered for miles."

In his later years David Wills lived in Greenwich and worked for the Wapping tug company, Alexander. He became the father of nine children, his daughter Irene being named after his old ship. He died in 1935.

THE MEMORIALS

A memorial service was held in the Dockyard church at Sheerness at 20.00 on 1st June which was attended by the Archbishop of Canterbury. The theme of the service was taken from the book of Joshua, "Be strong and of good courage." Most poignantly, a small piece of the ship's ensign was recovered from the beach at Sheerness that day.

The Lords of the Admiralty decided that the dependents of the lost Dockyard workers were eligible for the benefits of the War Compensation Scheme, this working out to be one-third pay for a widow and one twenty-fourth pay for each child. An immediate appeal was started locally and the "Guardian and East Kent Advertiser" published a poem by local man Henry Hall on 5th June which was subsequently reprinted (with, it should be added, a picture of the *Princess Margaret*) on thin card and sold for 2d in order to raise funds for the victims' families.

Every year on 27th May, a commemoration service was held at the Dockyard church and on the ninth anniversary in 1924, a carved oak altar frontal was dedicated by the Chaplain of the Fleet.

The *Princess Irene* is commemorated on panel 36 column 3 of the Portsmouth Naval Memorial on Southsea Common in Hampshire while the memorial opposite Sheerness railway station remembers not only the crews of the *Bulwark* and *Princess Irene* but also the 76 local Dockyard workers.

THE ENQUIRY - 1

One of the surprising facts concerning the *Princess Irene* disaster was that the Admiralty held the official Court of Enquiry as early as 10.00 on the day following her loss. The documents relating to this in the Public Record Office are marked 'Secret' and only became available to the public in 1966 after the statutory fifty year interval had passed.

The officers holding the enquiry were the Commander of HMS *Angora*, the Captain of HMS *Conquest* and the Rear Admiral in charge of HMS *Pembroke* - the Naval Base at Chatham.

The Court was of the opinion that the explosion was accidental and believed that this was probably due to a faulty compression 'pistol' if the striker projected into the primer so that it could penetrate the detonator when the primer was being screwed on.

The first person to give evidence had been Mr. Leonard Parsons of HMS *Angora* who was asked to explain how the mines were primed. His answer is extremely informative and gives an indication of the pressure that both he and others who carried out similar work were under. "In the ship that I am in, the Chief Electrical Artificer and the Chief Armourer cock the pistol and examine it. After that it is passed to the Torpedo Gunner's Mate - one Torpedo Gunner's Mate to each pair of mine rails. The priming party is stationed at a table between the mine rails, these men fitting the detonators into the primers. The fitted primer is then passed to the Torpedo Gunner's Mate who fixes it on the pistol, examining the pistol before fitting the primer. This is the routine carried out when we have time to do it, but as a rule, the thing is done at such a rush that you have to employ other people on the work in addition to the Torpedo Gunner's Mates."

Parsons was asked who the "other people" might be to which he replied "Leading Torpedo Men and Seamen Torpedomen." The Court asked whether these men would have had previous instruction and Parsons again showed his displeasure with the system by replying "Instruction in the ship" before going on, "the priming is practically the last thing done after the mines get on board and the men have practically worked 18 hours out of 24 and when it comes to the

priming they have just about had enough of it. Therefore unless you have got proper experienced people to do the work you cannot guarantee that the proper amount of care is going to be taken for the work."

Parsons was sure that the explosion was caused by a defective striker which, if the job were being rushed, could be prematurely fired.

Able Seaman William Paice was called next. He had been one of the three crewmen from the *Princess Irene* who were in Sheerness at the time of the explosion and was acting as the 'postman ashore.' Paice confirmed that he had left on the 09.15 'trot' boat and at that time the mines were being primed. All hands were involved in the task, he said. When the mines had arrived on board on Tuesday 25th May, all the pistols were taken in on the upper deck where the Carpenter's crew opened their boxes before they were cocked by the armourers who then stored them in the racks. On the following day, the working party from the Depot carried the pistols down to the men who were priming the mines.

Paice was asked if he had ever been involved in the priming of mines to which he replied, "Yes." He had assisted the Gunner in putting detonators into the primers and also assisted the Torpedo Instructors in cocking pistols. He also confirmed that the fitting of pistols was often carried out by men below the rating of Torpedo Gunner's Mate.

Paice was then asked whether or not he had any suspicion that there was any ill play in connection with the ship. He replied, "Three things happened in the ship some time ago and the Captain cleared the lower deck and said to the Ship's Company that he thought there was foul play going on in the ship. The first thing was the motor boat that was hoisted at the davits at night. The falls were turned up on the bollards of the motor and someone during the night switched on the motor but the cut-out of the motor went before the falls had parted.

Second: Someone had put a screw or nail between two electric wires in the Officers' Smoking Room and one of the officers happened to see the sparks flying from it.

Third: Someone had been into the engine room and switched on some valves that let water into the oil tanks." Captain Cobbe had gone on to say that these events could have been accidental but as they might have had serious results and they seemed to be a frequent occurence, it seemed advisable to warn the ship's company.

Paice stated that he had no suspicions of anyone on board to which he was asked, "All Englishmen as far as you know?" Paice thought that they were and in answer to a later question confirmed that the mine priming had started on the lower of the two mine decks. When he had left, there were three priming positions - some priming was going on in the upper mine deck aft and some on the lower deck aft with some forward.

Signalman John Sutton was the third witness and he too had been ashore at the fateful hour. He confirmed that at the time that he had left the ship, priming was taking place on both decks and that a party of between 80 and 90 men from the Chatham Depot were assisting the ship's company. They were carrying pistols about and taking off nuts on the tops of the mines. The 76 men from the Dockyard were working on the ship's two anti-aircraft guns and supporting the decks below the two mine decks with beams. This latter point is of interest as although the *Princess Irene's* builders, Denny's of Dumbarton, specialised in the building of fast, lightly constructed ships, the type of freight that she would have carried on the 'Triangle Route' would

certainly have not amounted to the weight of 400 plus mines and the stiffening that was taking place was to prevent the mine decks from sagging.

The next witness was Chief Petty Officer Thomson who stated that when he had left on the 09.15 'trot' boat there were, he reckoned, about 150 mines still to prime. His evidence must have horrified the Court as when asked whether to his knowledge the priming was being done in haste he stated that he thought the men were anxious to see how quickly it could be done. He had heard several men say so. A note of hidden humour came into the proceedings when Thomson (from Partick in Glasgow) was asked whether all the crew were English to which he replied, "All Britishers."

Mr. Stephen Quint, the Chargeman of the Sheerness Dockyard labourers on board was one of the group who were on their way back to shore when the explosion occurred. He said that his men had been drilling, rivetting and caulking at the time and that the upper stern mine rail was being tested. A mine and sinker (weight) were being lowered over the stern to check for clearance and Dockyard worker Samuel Clay had seen both Captain Cobbe and Commander Maurice inspecting this at 10.15.

During the course of the Enquiry, a defective pistol was actually produced as evidence. Found a few days previously in the *Angora*, its striker protruded more than one-sixteenth of an inch and would have instantly detonated any mine into which it was fitted. This evidence appeared conclusive but the Court also suggested two other causes both linked to the methods by which the mines were being primed. The penultimate paragraph reads, "Under the lamentable circumstances, the Court consider it is impossible to attribute blame but it is of the opinion that no plea of haste should ever allow these pistols being fitted by other than fully qualified men and further that a slight mechanical device should be fitted to the pistols to ensure that the pistol could not fire until it is properly placed with the other safety devices in the mine."

THE ENQUIRY - 2

Copies of the findings of the Official Enquiry were sent to a number of high-ranking Naval officers who in due time passed their reports back to the Commander-in-Chief, The Nore, Admiral Sir George Callaghan.

Writing on 1st June 1915, the Director of Naval Ordnance (DNO) considered that the prime cause of the disaster was down to a faulty pistol which was probably of little surprise to him when he wrote, "A danger from this cause has always been in view with the Heneage pistol and the consequent necessity for the greatest possible

HMS *Princess Margaret* lying at anchor in Portland Harbour during the period 1924-1926. Comparison with the trials views show a number of significant alterations to the original design. With a new and higher bridge, naval tops to her funnels, a modified stern area and a generally more cluttered appearance, the ship had lost much of her previous elegance. The minelaying ports can clearly be seen at her stern as can the guns below the bridge. *(National Maritime Museum, London. N21281)*

care has been repeatedly pointed out by (the) DNO. It is largely in consequence of this possibility (which however should never eventuate given great care) that the new pistol known as Mark IV has recently been proposed and approved for adoption on …17th May 1915. In this pistol the firing spring is not under compression till the proper moment of firing and the danger when priming is therefore reduced to a minimum. Manufacture has commenced and it is hoped in the near future to replace all pistols of the Heneage type. From the design of the Heneage pistol it is not thought possible to introduce a safety arrangement as it is proposed by the Court but it is for consideration whether any more Service mines should be primed with this type. It is pointed out that once primed the mines are very safe indeed and the only moments of real danger are between screwing the primer on to the pistol and introducing it into the mine."

The DNO found it "deplorable" that from the evidence given by Mr. Leonard Parsons of HMS *Angora,* seemingly irresponsible people should ever handle the pistol after it had been primed. It was even more deplorable he said, to read that "this business is done with a rush."

From this statement it is quite clear that the Navy were fully aware of the danger posed by use of the Heneage pistol. The fact that an order had been made to replace it with a safer version a whole ten days before the destruction of the *Princess Irene* indicates a lack of intelligence in the chain of authority linking those at the top who issued orders and those whose job it was blindly to follow their set procedures. They found their job both routine and tedious and readily involved unskilled colleagues in the task in order to complete it at their earliest convenience, seemingly oblivious of the dangers involved.

It is therefore quite possible that someone lacking sufficient experience in the priming of mines was encouraged to cock and load the pistols into the mines themselves. Unaware of the full consequences of loading a defective pistol, or even how to recognise the nature of such a flaw through familiarity with handling the items in question, the willing accomplice would have started a chain reaction. The explosion of one mine on board the *Princess Irene* may not have been enough to sink her but we must remember that most of the mines had been primed on the previous day and that on the morning of Thursday 27th May 1915, it was the final batch that was being made ready.

The Senior Officer in charge of the Mining Committee considered that if "proper precautions had been taken as those in TOG2214/15 of 1st March 1915 it is considered that an explosion from accidental firing of a pistol during the operation of priming could not happen." Furthermore he did not believe that the explosion was caused by a faulty pistol "as, if this were the case, the primer would explode while it was being screwed on the pistol and it could not then have been in the mine, which it is considered must be the case to cause the explosion of a mine." He believed that carelessness in seeing the pistol properly cocked before placing it in the mine was the primary cause of the accident.

Furthermore he stated that the Mining Committee, the DNO and the late Captain Cobbe had "all been aware of the great undesirability of retaining a pistol such as the Heneage type with a compressed spring and directed their attention towards obtaining a more satisfactory one." It was considered that the Heneage pistol should continue to be used until the introduction of the Mark IV type. "There may be a small risk," he wrote, "but it is considered not to be beyond the risks that should be taken at the present time." About 14,000 mines of this type had been laid since the outbreak of war and this was the first accident that had occurred.

He went on to say that the *Princess Irene* was due to sail on the morning of 29th May giving a whole three days for the mines to be taken in and primed. He did not believe that this showed any intention of requiring to rush the priming and found it difficult to understand just why, when three days were allowed in which to prime the mines, the 18 hour days as spoken of by Mr. Parsons at the Enquiry, were necessary.

He ended his report by recommending that additional Petty Officers be posted to the four HM minelayers *Angora, Paris, Biarritz* and *Princess Margaret*.

Finally the Commander-in-Chief, The Nore made his judgements. The fact that a number of witnesses at the official Enquiry had stated that the work of priming mines was often rushed (CPO Thomson of the *Princess Irene* had clearly stated that the men were seeing how quickly they could finish the work) and that, in order to accomplish this, untrained personnel were often used, did not make easy reading for those in higher authority and a 'cover-up' was inevitable. "The suggestion that the accident was caused by rushing the work is discounted" wrote M.J. Evans for the C-in-C.

In a further minute from the Fourth Sea Lord (dated 11th June) it was stated, "If no important operations will be interfered with, propose to suspend the use of the Heneage Pistol until a further report can be made … as to what is involved in waiting for deliveries of the Mark IV Pistol and how further use of the Heneage Pistol …. might be safeguarded - it being obviously undesirable to entirely suspend minelaying for any considerable period whilst at the same

time no similar loss of a ship such as this can be risked through an accident." It was further stated that "mines shall only be primed when the Minelayer is in a safe position as regards other vessels and shore surroundings; and secondly such an important operation shall not be left in the hands of Warrant Officers but must be carefully supervised by Executive Officers." The Third Sea Lord agreed with these findings.

Evans later wrote (on 21st June) that it was important to "correct any false impression" that the accident to the *Princess Irene* was due to Warrant Officers being employed on priming duty.

The DNO and Their Lordships duly concurred. The 'cover-up' was complete.

THE FITTINGS

On 19th October 1915, Denny's received a telegram from Major Kersey of the CPR which read as follows:-

"Can you advise me by letter of the price you could realise on behalf of the Admiralty for the fittings valued at five thousand to five thousand five hundred pounds 'Irene' stored with you?" On the following day, Denny's wrote to Major Kersey:-"We think we should state before we send you a valuation of the material referred to, that there are two ways of looking at the question. What we are adopting is, of course, the valuation of the material if it were replaced in the ship for which it was originally intended. This valuation will naturally bear some relation to the largely increased prices of the day as compared with the time of construction. If however, it be in your mind to get rid of the 'Irene's' material, and not use it in a vessel, then the valuation would naturally be what these parts would fetch in an open market. This would be difficult to compute, but in any case would be a very small figure compared with the other."

On receipt of the latter Kersey telegrammed back:- "'Irene': (the) value (of) this material would only be for sale or disposal in (the) open market as (it is) impossible now (to) consider (the) question of re-building (a) duplicate." [author's insertions and brackets]

This could indicate that following the *Princess Irene's* loss, the CPR did indeed consider building a duplicate steamer and at that time they still retained high hopes that both she and the *Princess Margaret* would eventually sail to the Pacific to take up the 'Triangle Route.'

THE *PRINCESS MARGARET*

At the end of the Great War all remaining merchant vessels which had been requisitioned by the Royal Navy were duly returned to their respective owners. All, that is, apart from one. The *Princess Margaret* was retained by the Admiralty after the demise of her charter on 27th April 1919 and in her minelaying role she was deemed to be both a very successful and almost ideal ship. During the period 1915 to 1919, no fewer than 59 minelaying operations had been carried out involving the laying of 25,242 mines.

Instead of sailing for the Pacific Northwest, she was purchased outright by the Royal Navy on 14th June 1919. She was immediately employed in the Baltic Sea in action against the Communist Russians and, in addition to laying mines, she also served as a refugee transport and hospital ship.

Then from late in 1921 until April 1923, the ship was refitted at Portsmouth and became an Admiralty yacht when she was used to carry guests of Their Lordships at the 1923 Spithead Naval Review. With her ample promenades, the steamer would have given her passengers an unrivalled view of the happy proceedings.

During November 1922 the Royal Navy ordered its first purpose-built minelayer from Devonport Dockyard. HMS *Adventure* carried 340 mines and was eventually commissioned in May 1927 at which time she replaced the *Princess Margaret* which was laid aside. Now surplus to the Navy's requirements, she was offered for sale.

The *Princess Kathleen* and *Princess Marguerite* had been delivered from John Brown's Clydebank yard in 1925 and with this new tonnage on the 'Triangle Route' the CPR had no obvious use for the 13 year old ship. And yet, during 1928, Captain Troop of the CPR was to advise his board in Montreal to consider buying the *Princess Margaret* in order to prevent her from falling into the hands of possible competitors on the Pacific Northwest coast. The rival Canadian National Railway (CNR) had bold ambitions to threaten the CPR's stronghold and so an inspection team crossed the Atlantic to scrutinise the 'Margaret.' It should have been no surprise that the ship had been well maintained but, although thought was given to using her on the summer Alaska cruise service, it was realised that the costs of rebuilding her passenger accommodation and refitting her (an estimated $1 million) would not have covered her projected revenue.

With the CPR's final refusal to purchase the redundant steamer in mid-April 1929, on 30th May the *Princess Margaret* was sold for a reported £14,000 to Blyth (Northumberland) ship breakers Hughes Bolckow & Co. On 2nd July she arrived there for demolition.

THE WRECK IN SALTPAN REACH

This seemingly should be the end of the *Princess Irene* story but that is far from the case. Immediately following the 27th May disaster, Royal Navy divers located the wreck and reported that they were able to walk around on the forward section of her "upper deck," stating that the middle of the ship had been blown outwards in an upward direction.

The day following the disaster the officer in charge of diving operations, Lieutenant-Commander W. Highfield, was able to inform his superiors, "Divers have examined the fore part close to No. 28 buoy and report what appears to be the upper deck is intact for a distance of about 40 ft., the bollards and capstan are also attached to the deck; abaft this the deck was partly collapsed. A large piece of the stem is showing at low water with the port bow plating attached but the starboard plating has been blown off. The ship's side below this deck has been blown outwards apparently as the diver can only feel jagged plating, One body was recovered forward found lying on the deck held down by some handrails. Several more bodies are also there held down by wreckage, also pieces of bodies. The chain cable can be recovered. The mast has been examined and it has a piece of derrick attached to it and is held down by twisted iron and beams; this is apparently the mainmast. Two of the obstructions well away from the ship were found to be flat pieces of plating lying on the bottom and are no danger to navigation. The three pieces of wreckage between No. 12 buoy and the wreck marking buoy have been examined and they stand about five feet off the bottom; this allows for a draught of 27 ft. at low water - the buoys have been left on those pieces. Between No. 28 buoy and the mast there is only a depth of about three fathoms at low water

The **Princess Kathleen** (pictured passing through the First Narrows at Vancouver) and her sister **Princess Marguerite** were built at the John Brown shipyard at Clydebank in 1925 for the "Triangle Route." They were the direct replacements for the **Princess Margaret** and **Princess Irene** although their design (three closely positioned funnels and counter sterns) represented an earlier period of shipbuilding. Both were to meet tragic ends, the 'Marguerite' was torpedoed in the Mediterranean in August 1942 while the 'Kathleen' grounded and was lost whilst cruising north of Juneau (Alaska) during September 1952. *(British Columbia Archives F-04400)*

and near No. 28 buoy where the deck is still intact only about six inches of water which gradually increases to about 10 feet."

On the following day two bodies were also discovered jammed within the wreckage whilst another body was found further aft and so tightly wedged than nothing could be done to free it. Although it had escaped mutilation, divers reported that its clothing had been blown to tatters. Lieutenant-Commander Highfield wrote in his second report to the Rear Admiral and Superintendent of HM Dockyard, Sheerness (dated 29th May) that "there is so much jagged plating and girders about that the divers are very much handicapped in their work as they cannot walk about freely." This was submitted to the Commander-in-Chief, The Nore with the hand-written addition from the Rear Admiral, "Every effort effort will be made ... to clear the wreckage of bodies but on account of the strength of tides, only a short time at slack water is available." The area was buoyed as early as the afternoon of the day of the explosion while protruding parts of the ship which posed a hazard to navigation were shortly removed.

Surprisingly perhaps, the *Princess Irene* was never declared a war grave.

THE 1960's SURVEYS

Passenger services to the railway station at Port Victoria were closed in June 1951 when the marshland immediately to the west of it was drained and cleared to become BP's Isle of Grain Oil Refinery. One of the tugs that latterly served the tankers at Grain was J.P. Knight's *Kenley* and in May 1962 it was reported that her towing wires had fouled an obstruction 1.5 cables south of Number 6 Jetty. The then Medway Conservancy Board subsequently carried out a close hydrographic survey of the site to reveal and locate the nature of the obstruction.

In July a diving survey was carried out over the main concentration of wreckage which discovered the river bed strewn with steelwork and distorted pieces of metal all in an irregular heap. The Admiralty was then consulted and a joint survey was conducted between 20th - 25th August 1962. During this time three badly corroded boilers, each measuring 14 ft. by 4 ft., were lifted. The maker's name was located and after requesting assistance from Babcock & Wilcox, a representative came to inspect the raised drums and associated boiler tubes. Once their numbers and test marks had been located, 3,883 on each of the tubes with the test stamp of 24th September 1914, it was possible to confirm that this was indeed the *Princess Irene*.

Further surveys and clearance continued throughout the following two years and the last major work in clearing the site took place in October and November 1964. The centre of the heaped wreckage was then about 4 to 5 ft. above the natural bed of the river and at this time over 25 tons of wreckage was raised both by direct recovery and by burning off obstructions. Side plating, inner bulkheads, stanchions, beams, frames, hatch coamings, tubing and heating pipes from boilers along with numerous smaller items were recovered. The completed work gave a final clearance of 29 ft. (8.8 metres) over the wreck at low water. It was noted at the time that the state of the wreckage removed clearly showed the effect of the explosion with very few large items being recovered intact.

Three particularly interesting items were recovered at this time. A brass letter 'E' from the ship's name together with a 15 inch porthole rim were removed from a section of side plating and together with a deadlight, these were presented to the Eastgate House

Museum at Rochester.

When the Grain oil refinery eventually closed in 1982 the site was again cleared and berths were constructed for the new container terminal which was named Thamesport.

THE BARGE

In October 1990, the remains of a large barge were discovered and removed from further up river and it was assumed that this had been moored alongside the *Princess Irene* at the time of the explosion. Although on account of the large lumps of coal which littered the river bed in its vicinity it was identified as a coal barge, the 'Irene' was an oil burner and at the Enquiry, the evidence given by Sheerness Shipwright Edward Standen indicated that the 'Irene's' barge was collecting discarded mine covers which were being thrown down into her from the steamer's adjacent mine decks.

Admiralty stamps from copper bolts in the coal barge's surviving timbers were found to date from March 1859 and it was believed that she was originally a man-of-war (possibly HMS *Forte*) which had been cut down at the end of her useful life in that capacity.

A further blow to the coal barge theory came in the form of a letter to a local newspaper in June 1995. The writer stated that his uncle had been the mate of the Goldsmith barge *Ada & Edith* which was on her way to deliver coal (presumably for galley stoves) to the *Princess Irene* at the time of the explosion. Witnessing the explosion and realising that nothing could be done, the barge went about and sailed back to her base at Motney Hill, her cargo intact.

The Official Enquiry into the loss of the *Princess Irene* lists a number of claims from barge owners whose vessels were damaged by the disaster in Saltpan Reach. Included in these is one for £650 from

The Sheerness Memorial to the 1,070 killed in the HMS **Bulwark** and HMS **Princess Irene** disasters of November 1914 and May 1915. It stands opposite the town's railway station. *(John Hendy)*

the owners of the sailing barge *Messenger* which was on Government charter and blown to pieces by the explosion. A further £300 was claimed on behalf of the barge's dead Master, Mr. Ernest Wakefield from Erith, who was on board his vessel at the time. His Mate, who was fortunately ashore, made a claim for £9 5s.0d in respect of lost personal belongings.

THE *PRINCESS IRENE* TODAY

The wreck of the *Princess Irene* remains on the bed of the River Medway, to the east of the present commercial container berths at Thamesport, and during the early months of 2001 its approaches were extensively dredged to allow larger vessels of deeper draught to dock there.

For some time the Medway Ports Authority had

been aware that the remains of the minelayer were obstructing the movement of ships using Thamesport's eastern berths but as they were unable to state categorically that all the mines and ammunition had actually exploded on 27th May 1915, no work had been able to take place to lift her remains.

Mr. Phil Woodgate, the Authority's River Services Manager, explains that the ship was moored over a shallow gravel terrace on the day of the explosion, at which time the decks below those on which the mines were stored (ie below the Main Deck - Deck D) were thrown down on top of it. The ship's keel, engine room and Orlop Deck (Deck E) would seem therefore to remain more or less in situ. Throughout the intervening years the wreck has been slowly buried beneath river silts and mud and in the words of the Harbour Master, Captain Peter White, "The visibility for divers and the silt covering the wreck has precluded close and detailed examination. Nevertheless we do have as much detail as present technology can provide."

In August 1997 a sonar survey was carried out over the wreck which clearly showed the remains of the *Princess Irene* as a bright yellow and red 390 ft. (120 metres) long anomaly with her stern pointing towards the south west and her bow to the north east.

Should at a later date Thamesport require expansion eastwards, Captain White considers that this will probably require the final removal of what remains of the *Princess Irene*..

CONCLUSION

The appalling disaster in Saltpan Reach was a precursor to the forthcoming carnage and slaughter on the battlefields of northern France and Flanders. Here men in their hundreds of thousands were also blown to eternity, their unmarked graves lying in a corner of Rupert Brooke's immortal "foreign field that is for ever England."

For the officers, crew and Dockyard workers of the *Princess Irene* whose scattered bodies and limbs were retrieved from the Medway and its surrounding marshes, theirs was a mass grave in Gillingham's Woodlands Cemetery.

And for all those who were not recovered, their final resting places became Burntwick Island, Grain Marsh, Stoke Saltings, Chetney Marshes, Deadman's Island and Slaughterhouse Point.

The Z1 buoy against the industrial background of the north shore.
(Phil Woodgate)

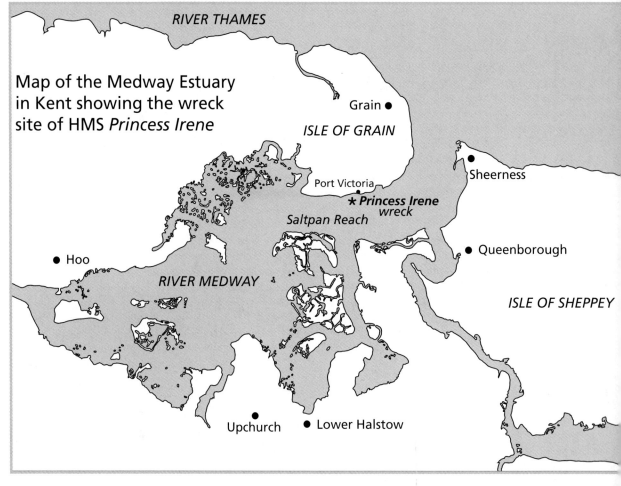

Map of the Medway Estuary in Kent showing the wreck site of HMS *Princess Irene*

RIVER THAMES

Grain ●

ISLE OF GRAIN

Port Victoria

Sheerness ●

★ **Princess Irene** wreck

Saltpan Reach

● Hoo

Queenborough ●

RIVER MEDWAY

ISLE OF SHEPPEY

Upchurch ●

● Lower Halstow